Dolphin
Coloring Book

Get FREE printable coloring pages and discounted book prices sent straight to your e-mail inbox every week!

Sign up at:

www.adultcoloringworld.net

ISBN-13: 978-1535537964
ISBN-10: 1535537965

PREVIEWS:

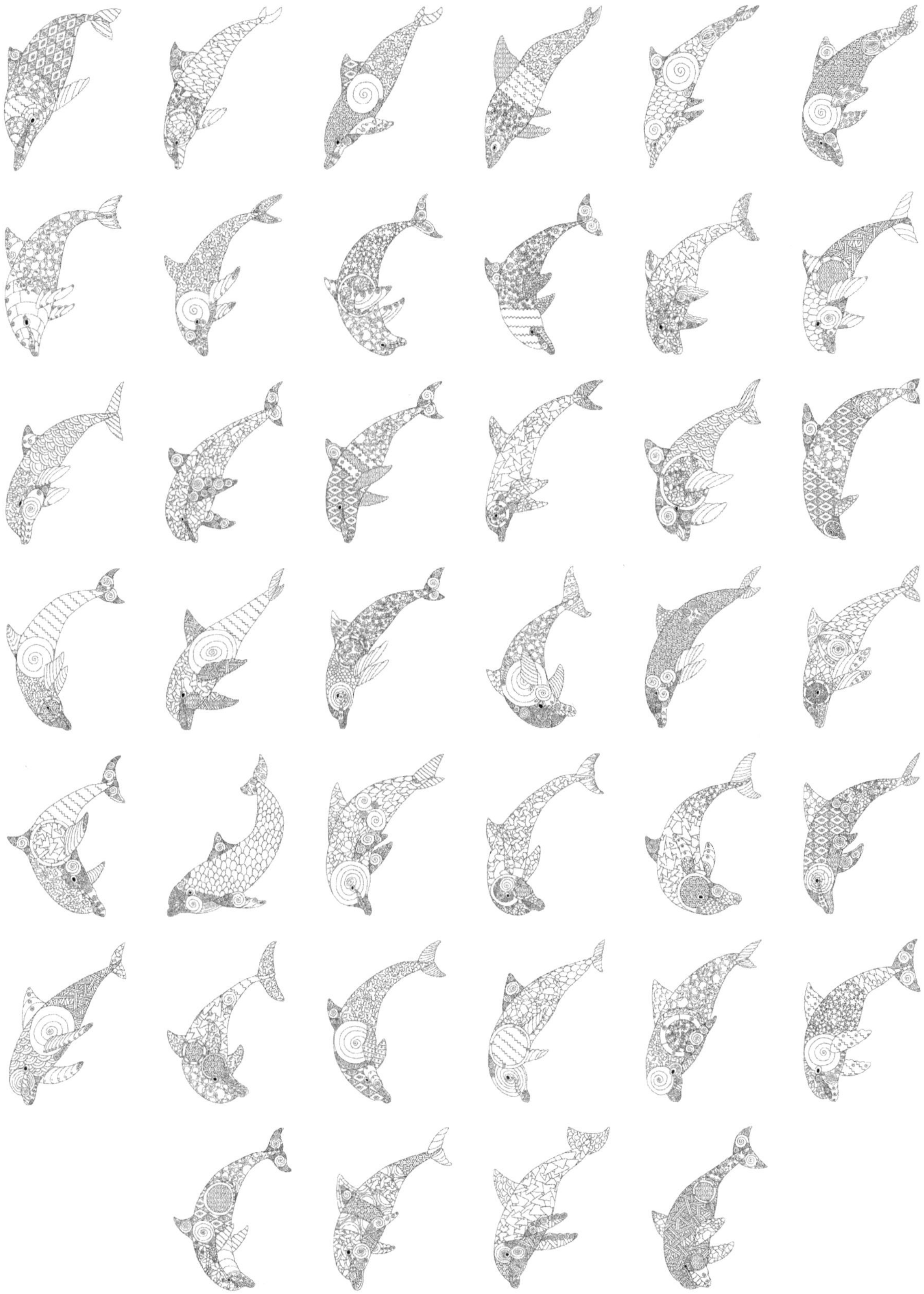

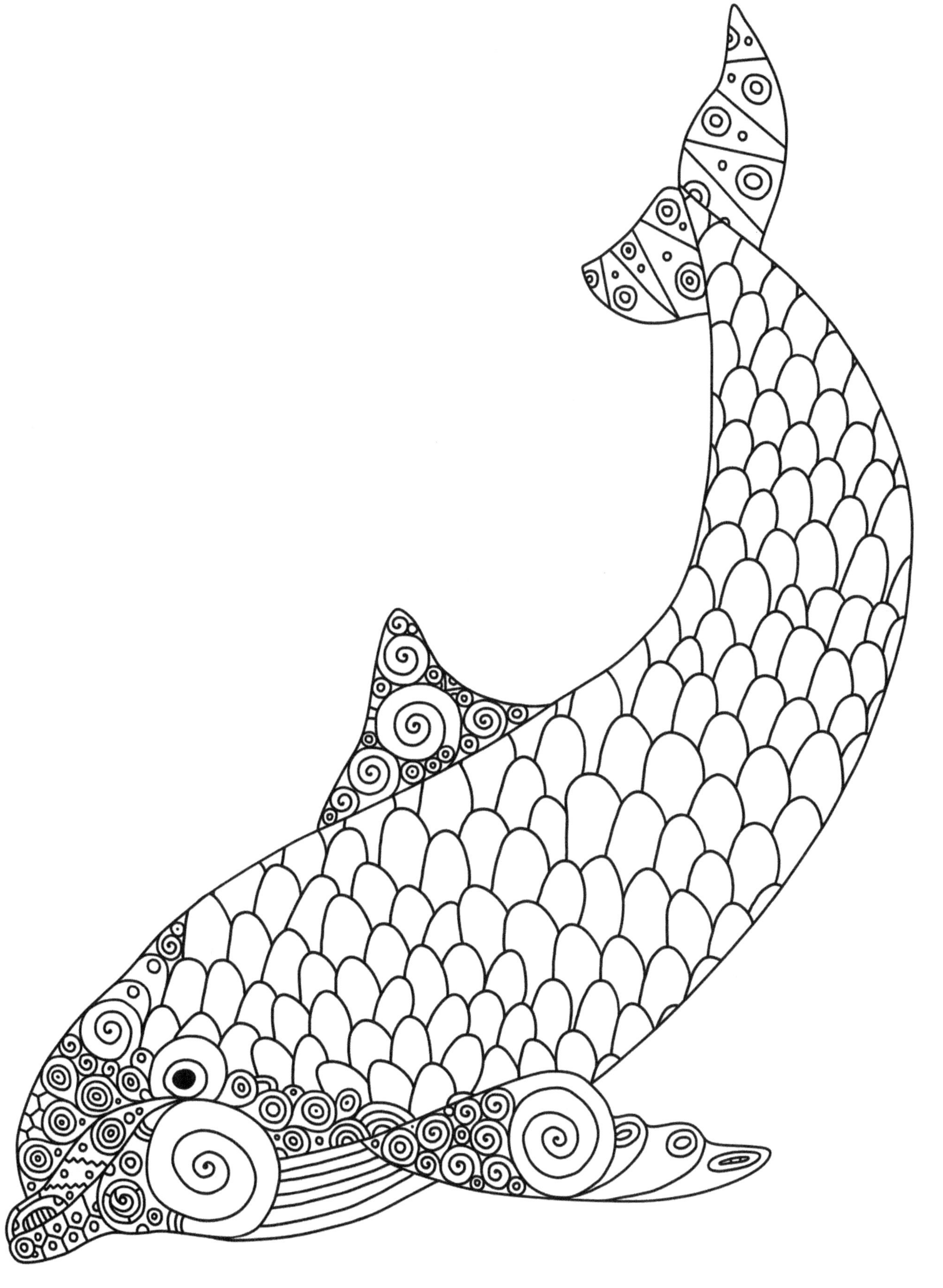

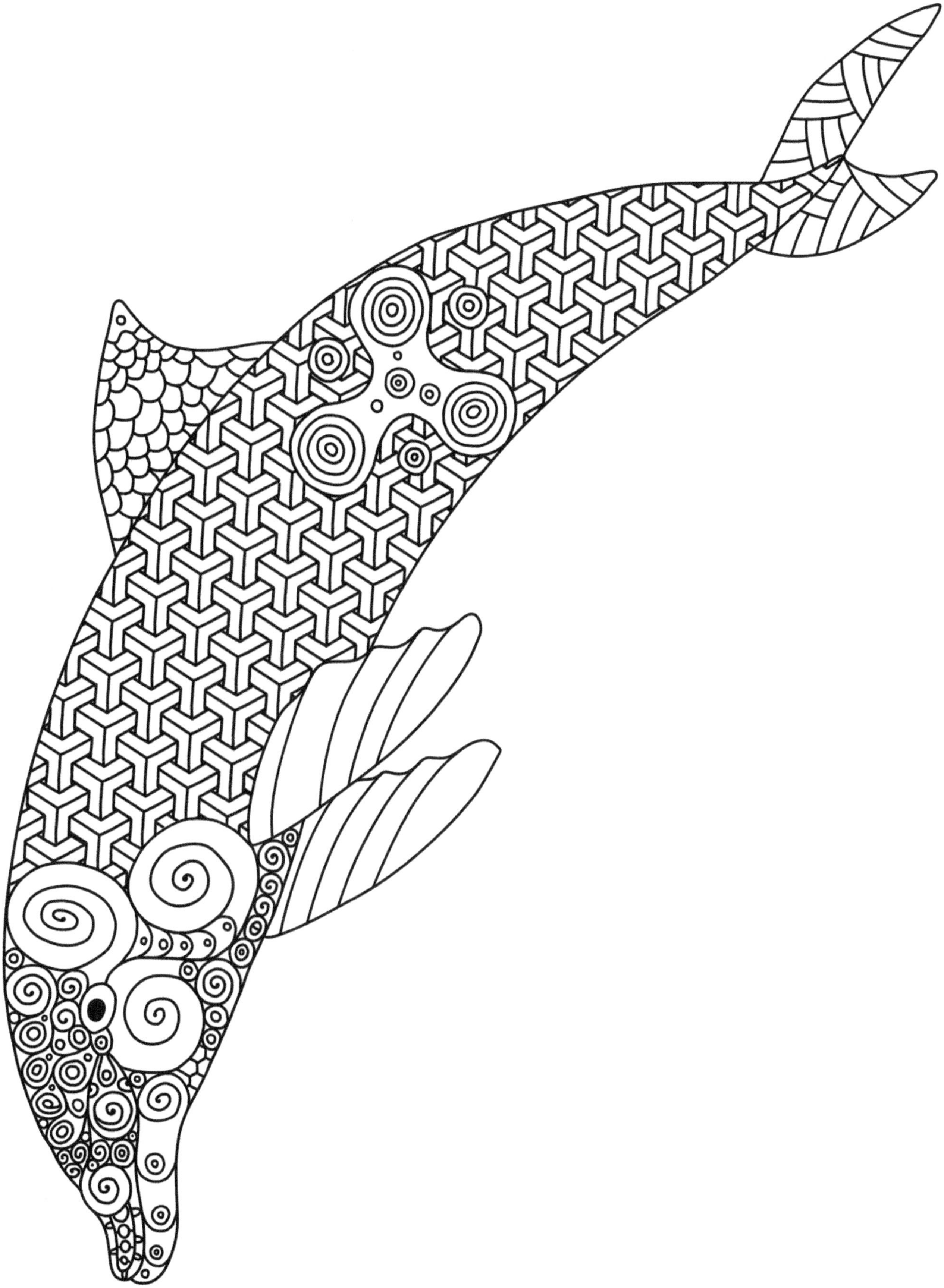

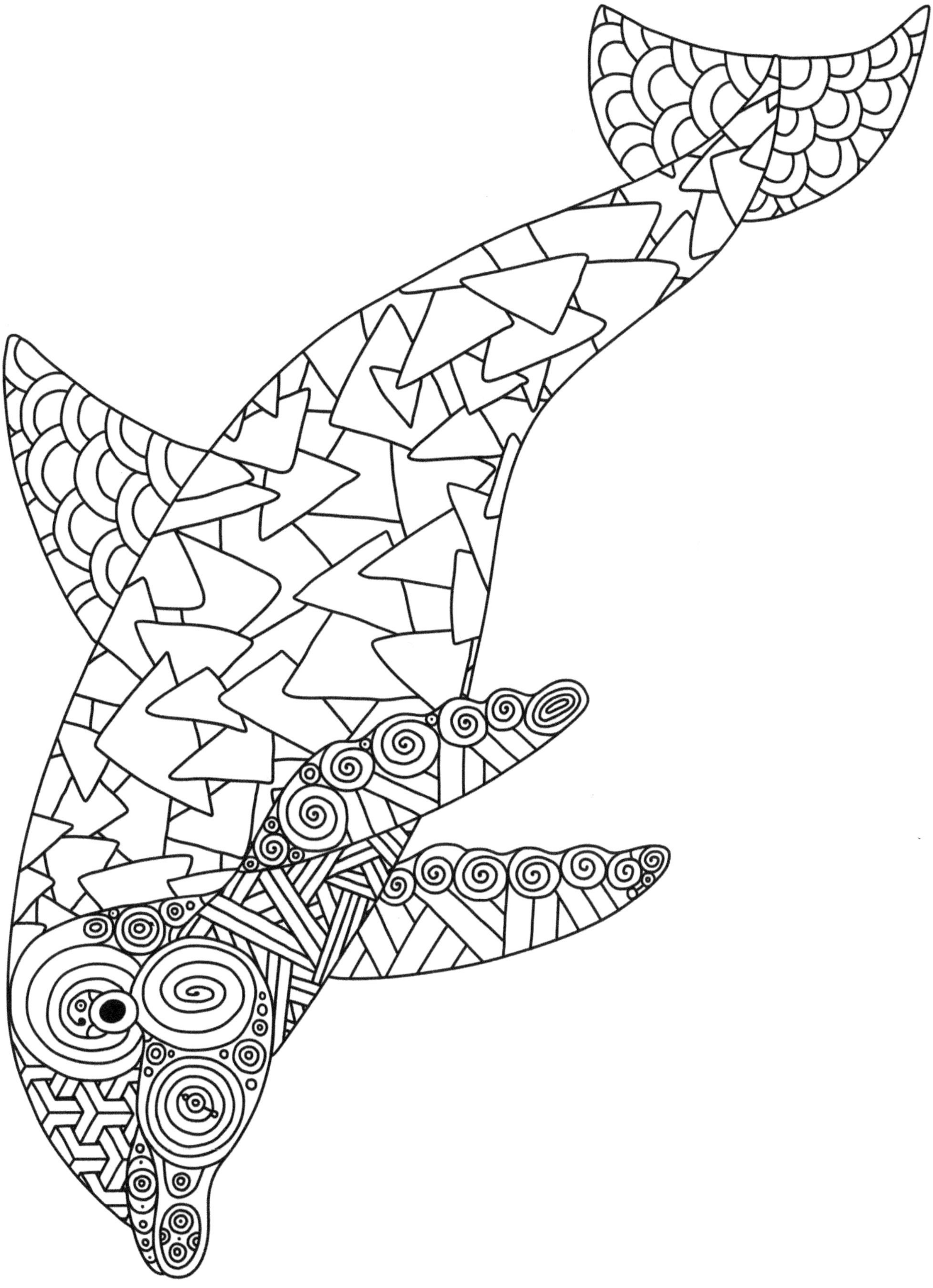

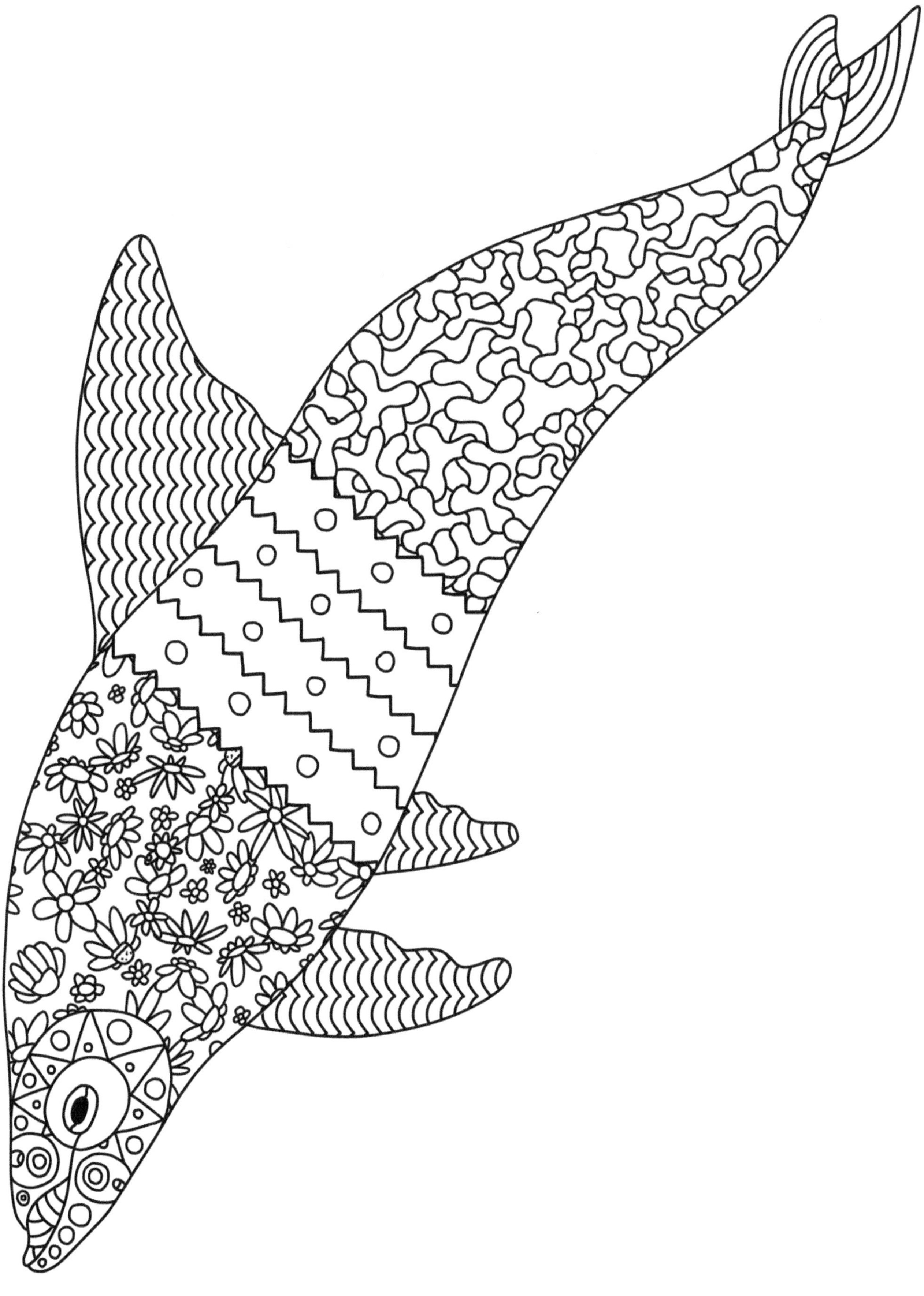

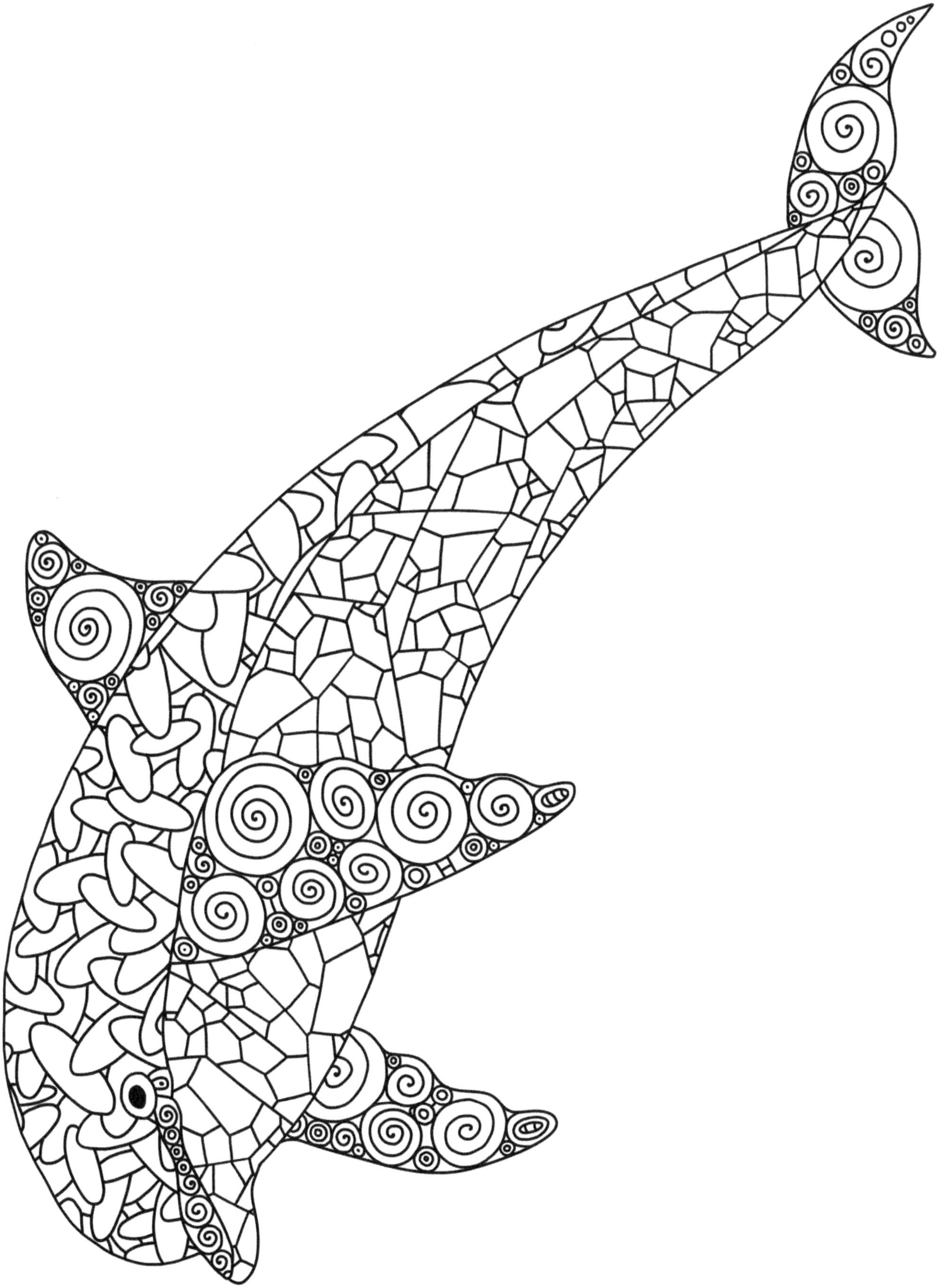

Color Test Page

Color Test Page

www.ingramcontent.com/pod-product-compliance
Lightning Source LLC
Chambersburg PA
CBHW052006280526
45793CB00005B/872
9781535537964